# IRVING'S ICKY
# INSECTS

# IRVING'S ICKY INSECTS

*Icky Insects! Who wants to look at them?*

*Irving does and he'll show you some of his favorites and who knows, maybe some of these icky critters will become your favorites as well.*

**Irving's Icky Insects.** Published by Caliber Comics, a division of Caliber Entertainment, LLC. Irving's Icky Insects is (c) 2016 Gary Reed. All artwork is the property of the respective artists included and (c) in their name and used for book reproduction only. No unauthorized reproduction of any contents in this publications is permitted unless expressly allowed by artist.

www.calibercomics.com

# IRVING'S ICKY INSECTS

**Written by:**
Gary Reed

**Irving Art by:**
Tony Miello

## Insect Art Contributors

Demone Amerson
Chuck Bordell
BJ Duvall
Jim Demick
Tom Finley
Craig Gassen
Robert Knight
Evan Kowalski
Trevor McKee
Stephanie Oz
Wayne Reid
Stephen Sharar
Tim Shay
Jeff Sornig
Adam Talley
Emily Zelasko

Hi! I'm Irving and I LOVE insects!

Some people find them icky but once you get to know them, they are kinda cool.

Well, maybe not all of them...
but most of them are.

There's so much to know about insects and scientists are learning new stuff every day!

Bugs, creepy-crawlers, pests...whatever they are called are a big turn off to some, but not to me...

...and maybe not to you once you learn more about them.

What makes up these critters?

They are a class called insects in the larger phylum grouping called Arthropods.

Insects have 3 body parts...
the **head**...
**thorax**- the middle part with the chest
and the **abdomen**...the stomach area

They have a single pair of antennae.

Craig Gassen

and all insects have SIX legs.

Count them...

1...2...3...4...5...6

So, that's why a spider is NOT an insect!

Yep, that's right.

Spiders are **not** insects even though most people think they are.

Spiders have 8 legs and only two body parts.

Remember insects have 6 legs and three body parts.

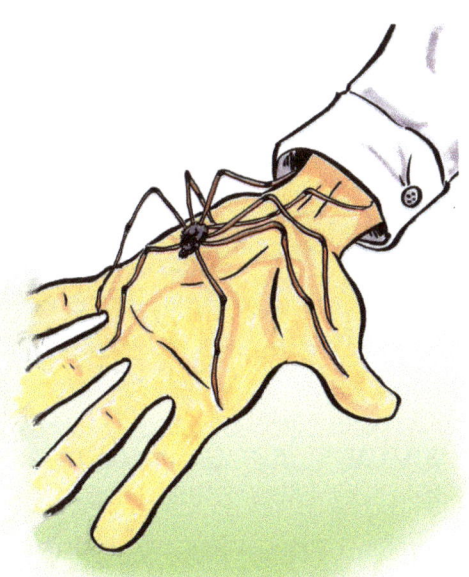

But a lot of folks still call them all bugs.

But only certain kinds of insects are really the bugs...but it is too hard to give the name of something crawling towards you real *creepy*-like.

People hate spiders but they actually help out around the house. They love to eat insects.

In fact, spiders eat more insects than all the birds and bats put together.

When spiders move, they always have four legs down on the ground at the same time.

They need all those legs and not just for walking.

Spiders have special hairs on their legs which are used for both hearing and smelling.

Mites and ticks also have 8 legs and are relatives of the spiders...or the **Arachnids**.

Most mites are really, really tiny.

You may not want to know but they like to crawl all over us.

And then there are the demodex.

They really like us.

In fact, most of us have them living in our eyelashes ...right now.

Don't look for them. They are really hard to see. And do you really want to see one up close?

And there's other bugs with LOTS of legs!

Centipedes and millipedes have a whole bunch of legs. That's why they can move so fast.

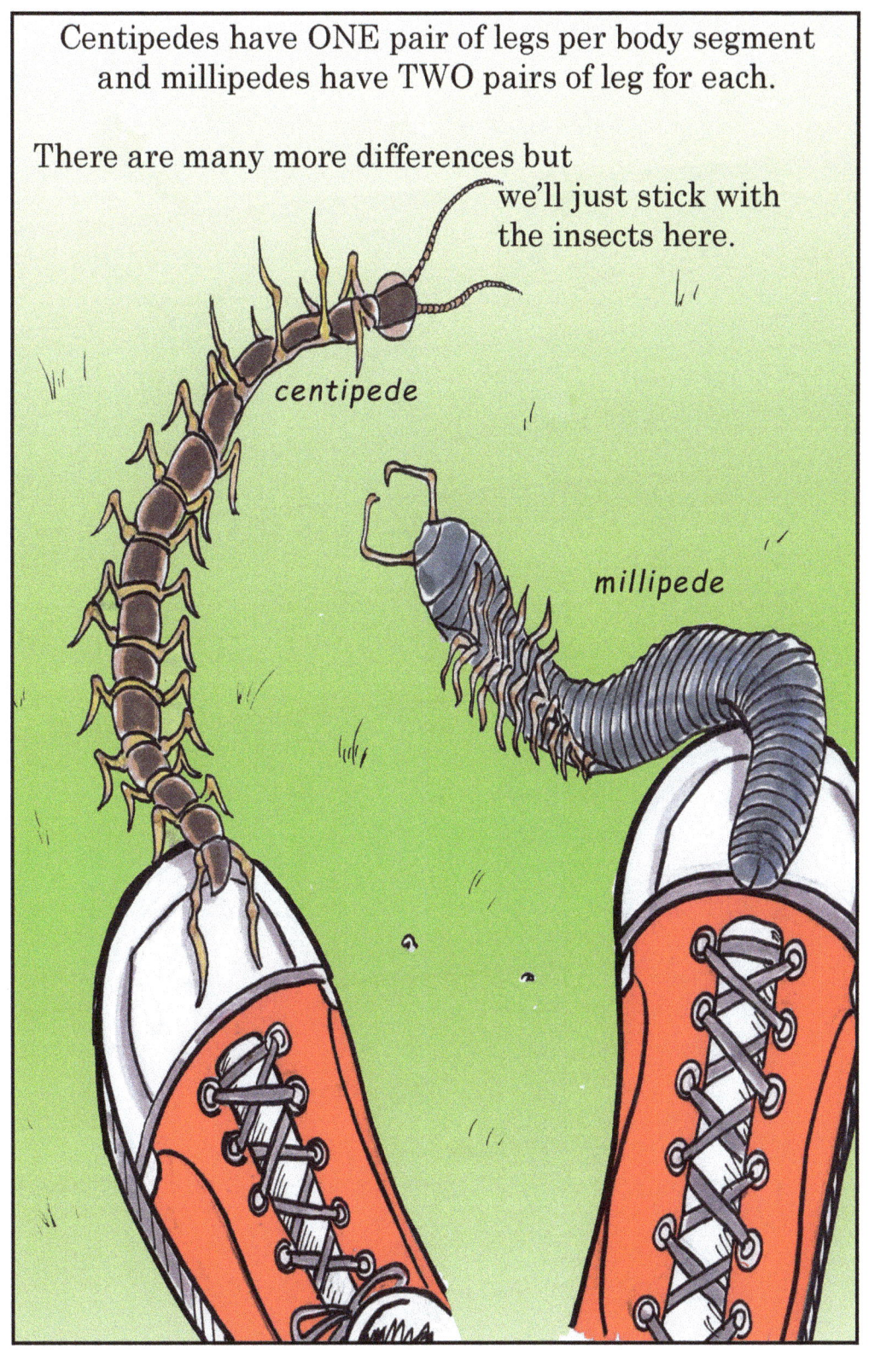

Many insects have a probiscus which is like a straw to such up juices.

And many of them have jaws or mandibles.

Some even have teeth.

In fact, the mosquito has 47 teeth but they don't ever use them.

Most insects have a pair of eyes.
but they are not like our eyes.

Our eyes are called simple eyes.

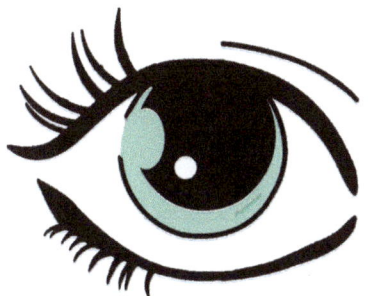 

They have compound eyes that are made
of lots of little eyes all put together.

And their eyes are big...really big.

This is what we would look like if we had compound eyes like most of the insects.

Insects come in all shapes and sizes.

Did you know most wasps are so small you never even see them?

And the Atlas Moth is so big, it is larger than many birds.

Most of the time, we think of blood as red.

Insects have different color blood.

Mosquitoes have yellow blood.
Cockroaches have white blood.

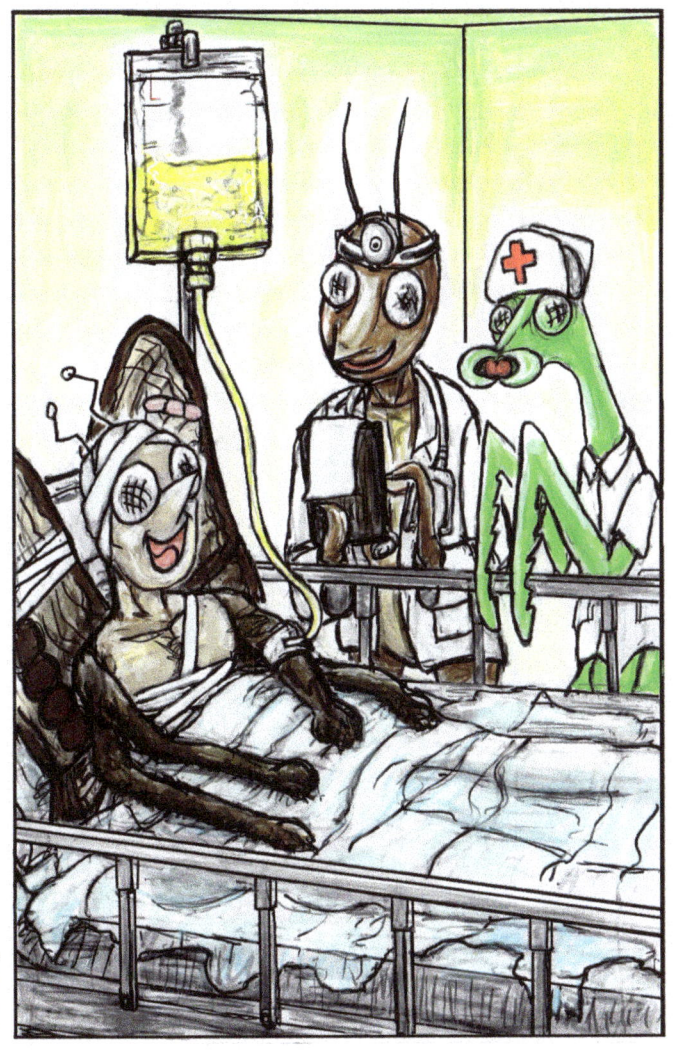

Insect relatives such as crabs
and lobsters have blue blood.

Insects can do amazing things!

Look at the flea.

If we had legs like them,
we could jump over
two football fields.

Dragonflies can fly up to 50
miles per hour.   As fast as cars.

Houseflies are slow pokes...
they can only fly at 5 miles per hour.

Most bees can fly around
15 miles per hour.

Dragonflies are amazing fliers.

They can fly straight up and down...

They can fly side to side...

They can even hover like a helicopter.

Dragonflies have to fly to eat as they catch their food when flying.

And they eat a lot of food. One dragonfly can eat up to 100 mosquitoes in just one day.

Dragonflies also have great vision.

They can see in front of them, the sides, and even behind themselves.

That's why their head is almost all eyes.

# Irving's Fun Facts

Entomology is the study of insects.

Entomophobia is the fear of insects.

Entomophagy is the eating of insects. Yuck!

People that eat insects say most beetles taste almost like apples. Wasps taste like pine nuts. Cooked larvae (the wormy like form before they become insects) taste like fried bacon. *Bacon!*

You know that hard coat on candies like sprinkles, *Milk Duds, Raisenettes, Goobers*, candy corn, and many others, is actually shellac made from the juice from bugs' butts?

There are many bug parts found in all sorts of food as it would be impossible to get rid of them all. So, the U.S. government allows so many in our food.

It is said that each of us eats almost two pounds of insects every year.

Yum!

That red coloring that you see in foods like yogurt, fruit cups, juices, strawberry drinks, and many more come from a dye called cochineal. Guess what?

Yep...it's bugs again. Cochineal is made from crushing up the cochineal bugs   Ewwww.

One of the most common insects are the ants.

It is said they make up the weight of
20% of ALL the animals on Earth.

Of course, we all know about the Queen!
She's the only one that can lay eggs.

One Queen can lay up to 300 million eggs!

I wonder if she names them all?

It is said that ants never sleep.
But they do.

Worker ants take short naps all the time.

Up to 250 times a day.

But the naps only last a minute or so.

I do that in school all the time.

Bees are like ants in that they always seem to be working. That's why they call them "busy bees."

One bee will get visit up to 500 flowers in one trip.

They need a lot because it takes over 4,000 flowers to get enough to make a teaspoon of honey.

Honey bees have two stomachs.

One is for their food and the other is to hold the nectar that they collect from flowers.

Bee eyes see different colors than we do.

The can see colors and shiny things that we cannot.

But bees don't see the color red.

That's why most red flowers are pollinated by birds instead of bees.

Poor bees...they don't have any ears.

Good thing though---I mean that buzzing noise would drive me crazy.

But think of all the good music that they're missing. They probably never heard of The Beatles...or Buddy Holly and the Crickets ...or the Bee Gees...or...

well, you get the point.

But bees do dance!

Emily Zelasko

They do what is called the
"Waggle Dance".

It is how they tell the other bees where
all the food is. They dance and use their
butts to let the other bees know what
direction and how far.

They also do a "Round Dance" but
that isn't as much fun.

Why are insects such as the house fly always attracted to the light?

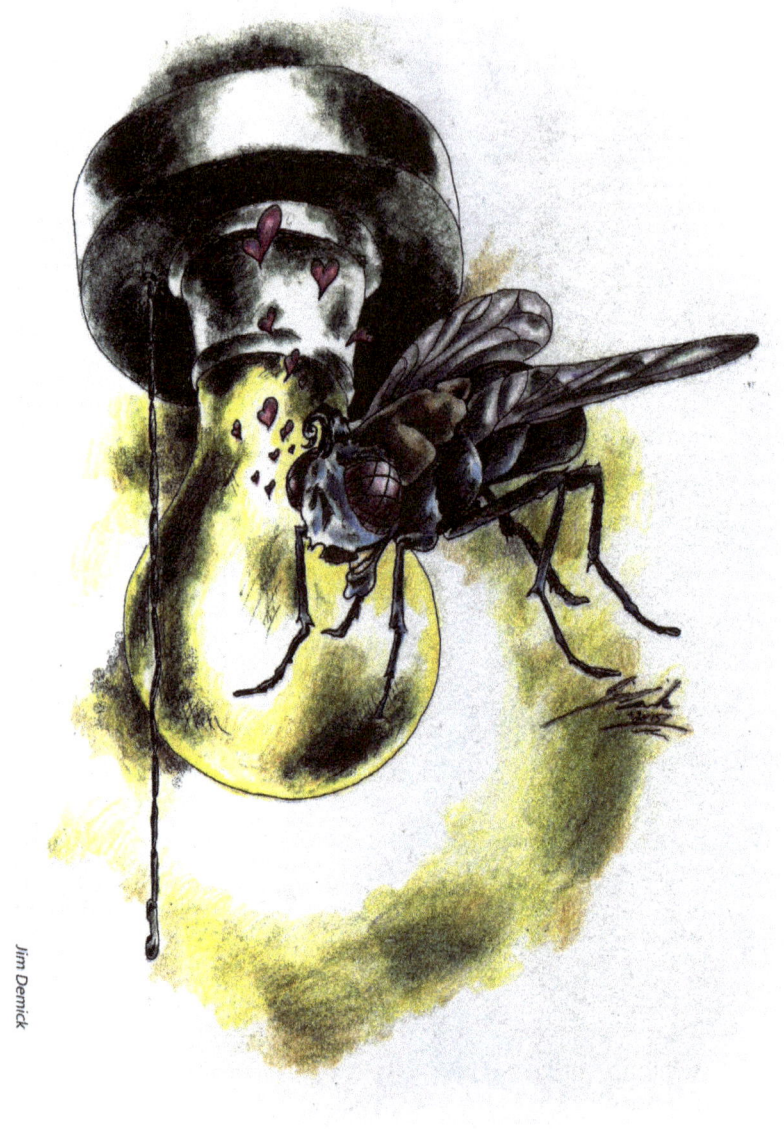

You know what? No one really knows for sure.

Maybe the insects think it is the moon.

Silly flies. Guess they are not too bright.

Even though most of us hate when flies are around us, some flies do good.

Like the Fruit Flies. Because of them, we've learned a lot about genetics.

Scientists use fruit flies all the time to study how genes work...that's the small bits of information that mom and dad pass down to their kids.

And we owe so much to fruit flies but I still don't like them around my bananas.

One of the weirdest flies is the Stalk Eye Fly.

The two eyes are on stalks far away from its head.

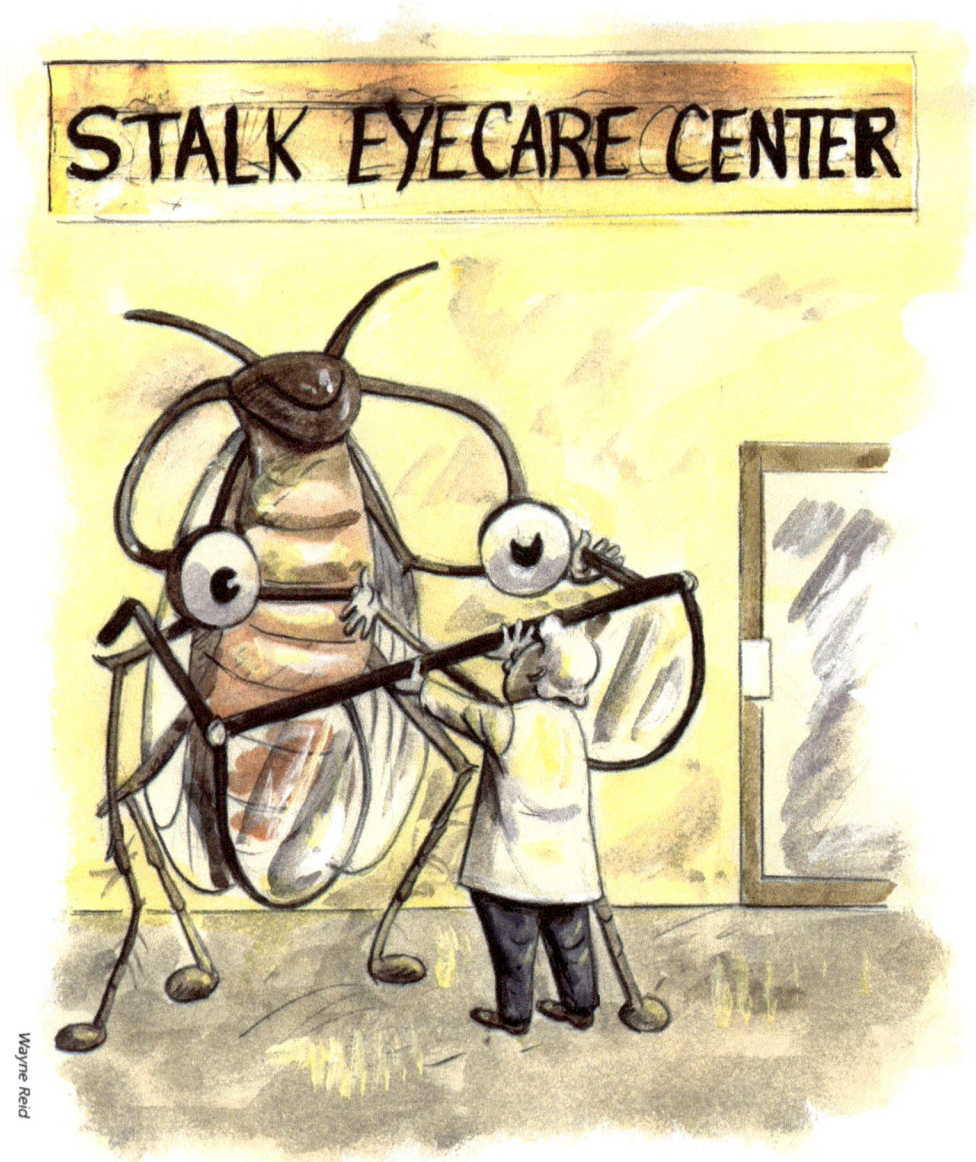

Why? Well, it seems that the girl flies like the boys that have their eyes furthest apart.

No one ever said flies had good taste.

Talk about growing up fast, the Mayfly becomes an adult after two years as a "baby" (or nymph) and then is only a grown-up for 24 hours.

That's a lot to get done in one day.

They probably don't take a lunch break.

So...just what is a "Daddy Long Legs"?

Some say fly, some say spider...

It depends. People call different things Daddy Long Legs.

Crane Flies which are flies...and Harvestmen which are *not* spiders...are both called Daddy Long Legs.

# Irving's Fun Facts

Each year, insects eat 1/3 of all the food that we grow.

For some reason, mosquitoes are attracted more to people who eat bananas and they also seem to like Type O blood.

Roly-Polys, or pill bugs, are famous for rolling up into a ball if you touch them but they are NOT insects but rather in the group Isopods, another type of arthropod.

We all know bees have those two big eyes but they actually have five eyes. There are three small eyes on top of its head.

Caterpillars have more than twice the number of muscles than humans do.

Houseflies "hums" in the key of F.

Centipedes always have an uneven number of feet pairs.

Female fireflies usually do not fly. Maybe they should be called "firesits".

Everybody likes the feel of silk.

Silk is made by silk worms which are the caterpillar form of the moth, *Bombyx mori*.

It takes a lot of silkworms to make silk. To get a pound of silk, enough to make a jacket, it can take up to 5,000 silkworms.

Good thing that all the mom moths lay about 300 eggs at a time and then off to work they go.

Butterflies, like almost all insects, do not have noses like we do.

So, to find out if something tastes good, they use their feet to smell and taste.

Just think if we did that!

Try it at home and see what your mom says.

Cocoons are why you don't see baby butterflies.

They are born as caterpillars and then spin a cocoon where they will change from that larvae stage to the adult form which is the butterfly or moth.

It doesn't seem like a lot of fun to be wrapped up like that.

What a way to spend childhood.

Stick Bugs are often called Walking Sticks because they look like, well...sticks.

That's how they hide from animals like birds and other insects that like to eat them.

Even though they can get very long, some almost two feet long, they still only have 6 legs.

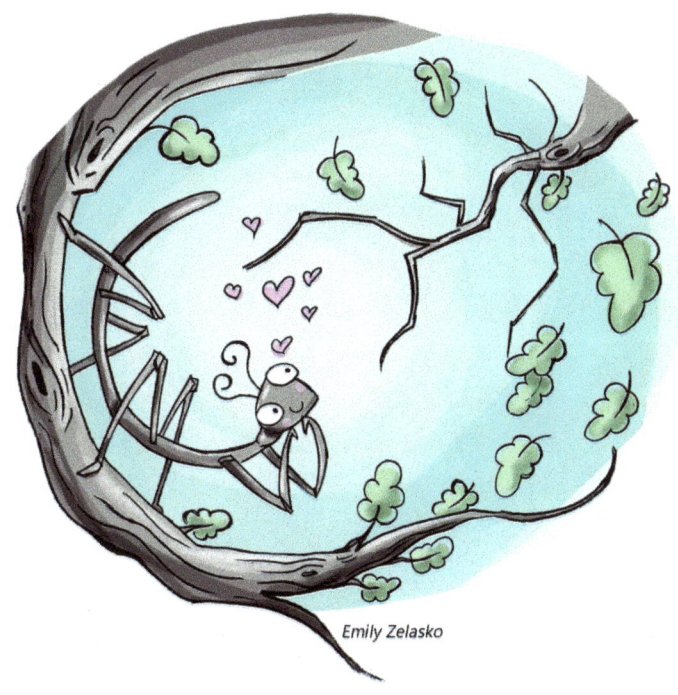

Emily Zelasko

Sometimes if they're caught by the leg, they just let it be pulled off as they can grow new ones.

Or if they're trapped, they fall to the ground and again, pretend they're a stick.

But they can also shoot our their blood which smells really bad so animals don't eat them.

Crickets chirping depends on the temperature.

Crickets chirp more when the temperature is warm.

In fact, you can tell the temperature outside by the number of chirps.

Add 37 to the number of chirps heard in 15 seconds and that will tell you the temperature outside.

Cockroaches are some of the oldest insects on the planet and also maybe the toughest.

They can survive almost anything...even losing their head. Yep, they can live up to a week without having their heads.

Now, that would be a great magic trick!

The Preying Mantis has two large eyes but only one ear.

The ear is on it's belly and can pick up the sound waves from the bats who try to eat them.

These are the only insects that can rotate their head so they can turn their heads completely around.

Pretty handy to keep track of what's going on behind you.

At first glance, you might think this is a grasshopper...but it's not. It's a katydid.

Katydids are actually more closely related to crickets even though they look like grasshoppers.

Grasshoppers have nubs on their legs which they rub to make noise.

Katydids, like crickets, make their sound by rubbing their wings instead.

Next time you are outside, take a magnifying glass and see how many insects you can find.

There are a lot of different bugs out there and sometimes you can find some weird ones.

Betcha you haven't seen too many of these!

The Giraffe-Necked Weevil found only in Madagascar.

These necks are really long on the males and they look scary but they only eat plants...in fact, they live almost only on one type of tree....the "giraffe beetle tree".

The Goliath Beetle is the heaviest beetle in the world.

Found only in Africa, it is in the family of the Scarab Beetles and luckily for us, it only eats plants.

In fact, it really likes sweet things such as fruit and sugary sap found in plants.

With such a sweet tooth, doesn't look like these Goliath Beetles will go on a diet any time soon.

This strange creature is the Brazilian Tree Hopper.

Look at those balls on top of its head.  Scientists think it is a way of making it hard for other animals to eat it.

Also, each ball has fibers which might be used for sensing the air vibrations.  Who knows?

Maybe they use them as Christmas tree ornaments and decide to keep decorated all year long.

Assassin bugs are a group that belongs with the nicer sounding "kissing bugs". But both suck blood and can carry bad diseases such as Chagas.

This type of assassin bug is unusual as it will collect dead ants and cover itself with them. It is thought that the smell of the ants wards off spiders which like assassin bugs but hate ants.

The thorn bugs are a type of treehopper and they have "helmets" on their heads that resemble thorns.

This makes them hard to see.

So, next time you grab a rose and feel a thorn, make sure you check to see if it is indeed a thorn...or maybe it just might be an insect!

These are called stink bugs.

So, why would they be called stink bugs?

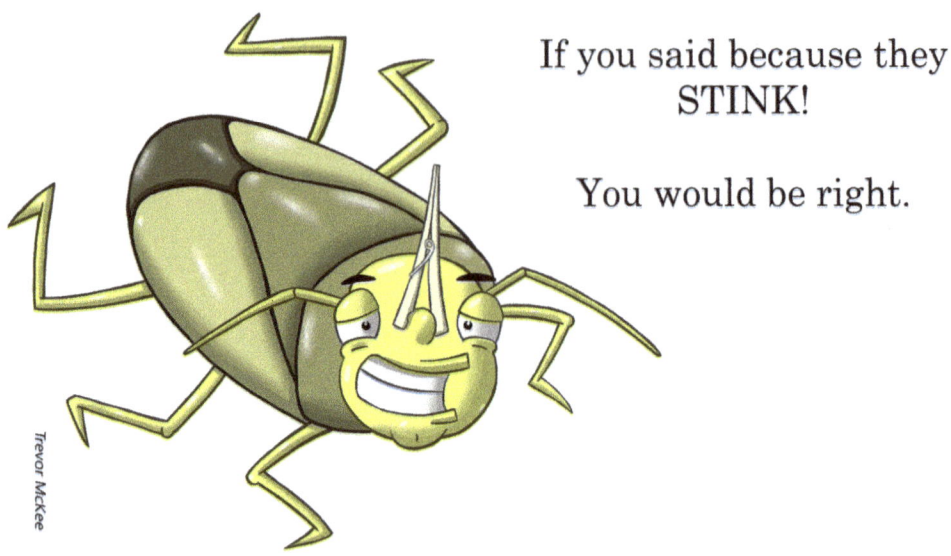

If you said because they STINK!

You would be right.

Stink Bugs give off a very bad smell when they are attacked. A lot of people say that the bug smells like old sweaty socks. Most of us know what that smells like!

But other stink bugs like the smell and that's how they attract each other.

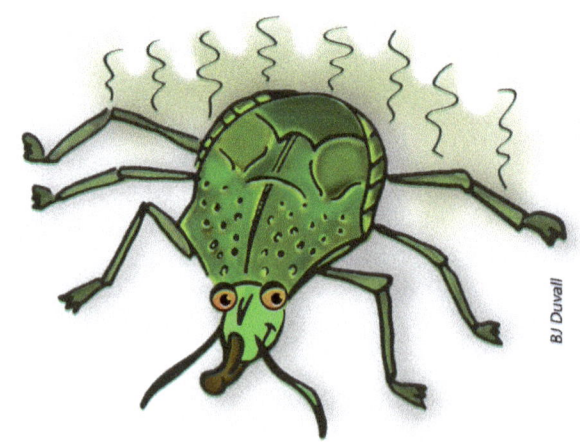

See I told you that looking at insects could be fun.

There's so much to learn about them and I am just getting started.

Time to look at more insects. There sure are a lot of different ones out there.

This could take awhile so I have to go now. Bye!

# If you enjoyed this book, be sure to check out Zelda's Zombie Zoo.

Join Zelda, a caretaker for a very special zoo...a zombie zoo! All the animals are zombies, except her cat, Meow, so that makes things a bit different and a little odd. But Zelda has all sorts of fun facts to share with young readers about zoo animals.

# DRAW YOUR OWN FAVORITE INSECT HERE

www.ingramcontent.com/pod-product-compliance
Lightning Source LLC
Chambersburg PA
CBHW061226070526
44584CB00029B/3999